Ninety-Second
Brainteasers

ALAN STILLSON

Official
American Mensa
Puzzle Book

Sterling Publishing Co., Inc.
New York

For Gail
and our ever-supportive family

Copyedited by Liz Kaufman
Designed by Jeff Fitschen

Library of Congress Cataloging-in-Publication Data Available

10 9 8 7 6 5 4 3 2 1 ·

Published by Sterling Publishing Co., Inc.
387 Park Avenue South, New York, NY 10016
© 2003 by Alan Stillson
Distributed in Canada by Sterling Publishing
^c/o Canadian Manda Group, One Atlantic Avenue, Suite 105
Toronto, Ontario, Canada M6K 3E7
Distributed in Great Britain by Chrysalis Books
64 Brewery Road, London N7 9NT, England
Distributed in Australia by Capricorn Link (Australia) Pty. Ltd.
P.O. Box 704, Windsor, NSW 2756, Australia

Sterling ISBN 0-8069-9393-6

CONTENTS

INTRODUCTION

Ninety-Second Brainteasers was written to provide continuing enjoyment to *One-Minute Brainteasers* fans and to attract new readers to the delights of short, thematic no-pencil puzzles. This book will introduce new themes as well as utilize some of the themes used in the original book.

You can solve most of these puzzles within ninety seconds. This allows you, the busy thinker, to control and time your mental workouts. Every puzzle can be solved independently. You can begin and end wherever and whenever you wish. When you're ready for more exercise, simply pick up where you left off.

With a trivia question, you either remember the fact or you do not. A brainteaser coaxes a little thought; it teases you into constructs or concepts of your own. We like to think of it as a kind of breezy mental gymnastics that's great fun.

How hard are these puzzles? A Mensa puzzle panel tested every brainteaser. You can compare your results with American members of Mensa. These are people who have an I.Q. in the top two percent of the American population. Panel members solved about sixty percent of the puzzles correctly. Of course, results varied from one group of puzzles to another.

Some puzzles may have alternate solutions that we didn't find. Evaluate your results accordingly.

This book is divided into five parts: "Quick Word Puzzles," "Something in Common," "In the Store," "Hidden Places," and "Name Games." In the fifth part, "Name Games," you can earn bonus points.

Ready to rev up your mental motor? Here's your green light. Sixty-nine members of American Mensa, Ltd. volunteered to be members of the testing panel for *Ninety-Second Brainteasers.* They received the puzzles by e-mail with instructions to take no more than about ninety seconds per puzzle. When they sent back their answers, we tabulated the results, rounding off the percentage of correct answers to the nearest five percent for each group of puzzles and for the whole book.

American Mensa Puzzle-Testing Panel

I'd like to give special thanks to members of the Mensa puzzle-testing panel for this book: Ilene Hartman-Abramson, Ph.D.; Jim Achuff; Dean A. Beers; Nancy Beringer; Brandi Besalke; Walter W. Beveridge, M.S.; Laurie Anne Bradford; Rick Brooks; Howard Bryks; Jody Carlson; David Cohen; Karen J. Cooper; Darrell Costello; Ben Curtis; Dennis J. De Balso; Joe Devney; Patricia Donohue; Chris Dudlak; George Dunn; Jonathan Elliott; Ted Elzinga; George A. Fagan; Rita Foudray; Sande Frisen; Ltc. Thomas G. Funk (Ret.); John Furkioti; Ann M. Garbler; Pete Gouvitsas; Steve High; Alan Hochbaum; Eric Holmquist; Ronald M. Kupers, CPA; Steve Latterell; Victor I. Lee; Dirk C-J Lenhart; David Linko; Dennis A. Littlefield; Elaine Loughrey; Donald Mann; Alan Mesch; Mary Lu Michell; John Mochan; Charles T. Murphy; Sandra J. Nelson; Frank Anthony Oblak; John P. "Jack" Ray; Donald Richmond; Mary Lou Robinson; Diane Rozek; Steve Schwartzberg; Ronald M. Sharma; Bill Siderski (with help from his 10-year-old son, Kyle); Deborah R. Smith, Ph.D.; Laura M. Sprow; Heather Stewart; Tomothy J. Sullivan; Jim Tasker; Bethany Thivierge; Dennis Tomlinson; Selena M. Updegraff; Stephen Vincencio; Andrea Wainwright; Wendy Jackson Walker; Mitchell I. Weisberg; Markell Raphaelson West; Darrin M. Wiederhold, DMD; Andrea Williams; John K. Woodlock.

There's an extra tip of the hat for Jonathan Elliott, George A. Fagan, and Heather Stewart for offering extensive editorial suggestions.

About the Author

Alan Stillson's puzzles have appeared in *American Way*, the American Airline in-flight magazine. He is puzzle editor for Greater Los Angeles Mensa and provides puzzles to local Mensa publications throughout the United States. His puzzle books, *One-Minute Brainteasers*, *The Mensa Genius ABC Quiz Book*, and *Match Wits with Mensa*, co-authored with Marvin Grosswirth and Dr. Abbie Salny, continue to delight readers. His puzzles have been reviewed in *People* magazine. Mr. Stillson is a member of Mensa, the National Puzzlers League, and the National Scrabble Association.

Part I

QUICK WORD PUZZLES

Answers are on pages 76–82.

Movies–2000 & Beyond

A mysterious creature known as the Letter Monster has devoured the middle letters of several movies from 2000 and beyond. For example, *The Mummy Returns*, 2001, starring Brendan Fraser, has become *T __ E M __ __ __ Y R __ __ __ __ __ S*. Find the original titles of these movies before the Letter Monster got to them.

1. *E __ __ N B __ __ __ __ __ __ __ __ H, 2000*, starring Julia Roberts

2. *P __ __ __ L H __ __ __ __ R*, 2001, starring Ben Affleck

3. *R __ __ __ __ __ __ R T __ E T __ __ __ __ S*, 2000, starring Denzel Washington

4. *H __ __ __ __ __ __ L*, 2001, starring Anthony Hopkins

5. *H __ __ __ T*, 2001, starring Gene Hackman and Danny DeVito

6. *F __ __ __ __ __ G F __ __ __ __ __ __ __ R*, 2000, starring Sean Connery

7. *D __ __ __ __ __ __ C D __ __ __ __ __ __ __ __ __ E*, 2001, starring John Travolta

8. *S __ __ __ __ __ __ __ __ Y*, 2001, starring John Cusack

9. *G __ __ __ __ __ __ __ R*, 2000, starring Russell Crowe

10. *Z __ __ __ __ __ __ __ R*, 2001, starring Ben Stiller

Answers are on page 76.

Movies–2000 & Beyond

11. _W _ _ T W _ _ _ N W _ _ T,_ 2000, starring Mel Gibson

12. _T _ _ _ _ _ _ G D _ Y,_ 2001, starring Denzel Washington

13. _H _ _ _ _ S IN A _ _ _ _ _ _ S,_ 2001, starring Anthony Hopkins

14. _M _ _ S C _ _ _ _ _ _ _ _ _ _ Y,_ 2000, starring Sandra Bullock

15. _B _ _ _ K K _ _ _ _ T,_ 2001, starring Martin Lawrence

16. _R _ _ _ _ _ _ R G _ _ _ S,_ 2000, starring Ben Affleck

17. _S _ _ _ K,_ 2001, starring Mike Myers

18. _H _ _ _ _ _ _ L,_ 2001, starring Keanu Reeves

19. _C _ _ _ _ _ _ _ G T _ _ _ R, H _ _ _ _ N D _ _ _ _ N,_ 2000, starring Yun-Fat Chow

20. _A _ _ _ _ _ T F _ _ _ _ S,_ 2000, starring Kate Hudson and Billy Crudup

Answers are on page 76.

Movies–the 1990s

Several movies from the 1990s have suffered a similar fate. For example *Air Force One*, 1997, starring Harrison Ford, has become *A __ R F __ __ __ E O __ E*. Find the original titles of these movies.

1. *R __ __ H H __ __ R*, 1998, starring Jackie Chan and Chris Tucker

2. *D __ __ __ H B __ __ __ __ __ S H __ R*, 1992, starring Meryl Streep and Goldie Hawn

3. *T __ E H __ __ __ __ __ __ __ E*, 1999, starring Denzel Washington

4. *B __ __ __ G J __ __ N M __ __ __ __ __ __ __ H*, 1999, starring John Cusack

5. *P __ __ __ __ Y W __ __ __ N*, 1990, starring Julia Roberts

6. *A __ __ __ __ __ E T __ __ S*, 1999, starring Robert DeNiro

7. *H __ __ P D __ __ __ __ S*, 1994, starring William Gates

8. *A __ __ __ __ __ __ __ __ N*, 1998, starring Bruce Willis

9. *R __ __ __ __ __ __ Y B __ __ __ E*, 1999, starring Julia Roberts

10. *P __ __ __ __ __ __ __ __ __ __ A*, 1993, starring Tom Hanks

Answers are on page 77.

Movies–the 1990s

11. *S _ _ _ G B _ _ _ E*, 1996, starring Billy Bob Thornton

12. *D _ _ _ _ E J _ _ _ _ _ _ Y*, 1999, starring Tommy Lee Jones

13. *F _ _ _ O*, 1996, starring William H. Macy

14. *G _ _ _ _ Y Q _ _ _ T*, 1999, starring Tim Allen and Sigourney Weaver

15. *P _ _ P F _ _ _ _ _ N*, 1994, starring John Travolta and Bruce Willis

16. *T _ _ E L _ _ S*, 1994, starring Arnold Schwarzenegger

17. *T _ _ _ E K _ _ _ S*, 1999, starring George Clooney

18. *J _ _ _ Y M _ _ _ _ E*, 1996, starring Tom Cruise

19. *H _ _ _ Y G _ _ _ _ _ E*, 1996, starring Adam Sandler

20. *T _ E U _ _ _ L S _ _ _ _ _ S*, 1995, starring Stephen Baldwin

Answers are on page 77.

MENSA SCORING	
Average Mensa Score:	70%

Half-Eaten Foods

In this puzzle, every other letter of certain foods is missing, leaving no blanks to indicate where letters have been removed. Sometimes, the odd-number letters are missing; at other times, the even-number letters have been removed. For example, SPAGHETTI has become SAHTI. Discover what the foods were before the letters were removed.

1. SAAU
2. TRIL
3. OTROS
4. OEDW
5. GAERI
6. AEKAT
7. CSEOE
8. AALOE
9. TABRY
10. RNFRE

11. COOAE
12. AEPEFR
13. TMUA
14. OAG
15. UQA
16. HRIG
17. AEMLN
18. URT
19. ECRO
20. DUHU

Answers are on page 77.

MENSA SCORING

Average Mensa Score:	50%

Half-Eaten Occupations

This time, half of the names of occupations are missing. Once again, the odd-number letters may be gone; at other times, the even-number letters are missing. For example, a PHYSICIST becomes HSCS. Find out what the occupations were before the letters were removed.

1.	WETE	**11.**	OPRLE
2.	SAITCA	**12.**	ATAY
3.	HRPATR	**13.**	TEPA
4.	AEDSE	**14.**	OSLAT
5.	ILNS	**15.**	PYHLGS
6.	MTOOOIT	**16.**	PIATRPS
7.	ETERNU	**17.**	HTGAHR
8.	ADOD	**18.**	AIEMS
9.	RFSO	**19.**	IITR
10.	PEIET	**20.**	SLIR

Answers are on page 78.

A-Team Puzzles

The letter "A" is extremely versatile. It can team up in front of a word with a space as an article, and it can team up in front of certain words without a space to form a new word. In some cases, it can team up both ways in the same sentence. For example, the sentence "_____ with influenza is usually over in _____ seven days" makes sense using A BOUT and ABOUT. Try to send in your A teams to make sense out of these sentences.

1. Find _____ to put all your clothes _____.

2. He wanted to _____ for the many times his voice had _____ of sarcasm.

3. The more you let your body _____, the harder it will be to win _____ in any sport.

4. There was much _____ after the diva ended on a *ti* instead of _____.

5. Someone suggested _____ for next year's advertisers convention on Madison _____.

6. The fly scorched its wings when it _____ on _____ match.

7. The mobster made _____ that his girlfriend would _____ him.

8. Most children _____ three years old have learned that you can't put a square peg into _____ hole.

9. The manager tried to _____ his pitchers every time they allowed _____ to be stolen.

10. Is it necessary to use _____ bridge to get to the _____?

Answers are on page 78.

A-Team Puzzles

11. All kidding _____, $1,500 is too much to pay for _____ of beef.

12. He noticed _____ of ozone during his _____ of Mount Everest.

13. The difference between an astronomer and a chemist is studying an _____ versus studying _____.

14. _____ check should be _____.

15. While eating _____ dog, he saw a squirrel with an _____.

16. The project was given _____ a long time _____.

17. It will probably take _____ time for the feuding neighbors to learn to get _____ with each other.

18. Do poets still _____ themselves with stories of how _____ inspired their writing?

19. When she _____, she realized that _____ bush had been damaged during the overnight storm.

20. Is _____ of the court allowed to receive an _____ for damages?

Answers are on page 78.

MENSA SCORING

Average Mensa Score:	80%

Word Chains

Some six-letter words end in three-letter groups that can be used to start a second six-letter word. Sometimes, the last three letters of the second word can start a third six-letter word. On rare occasions, the last three letters of the third word can start a fourth six-letter word. One example of this is ZIRCON – CONFER – FERVID – VIDEOS.

Try to find a second and third six-letter word to complete these word chains (watch for some uncommon spellings).

1. CUTLET – _____ – _____ – MEDIAN

2. MADCAP – _____ – _____ – IODINE

3. SORBET – _____ – _____ – QUEUES

4. GRAHAM – _____ – _____ – OXYGEN

5. GROUSE – _____ – _____ – CRAFTY

6. MUSCAT – _____ – _____ – PERSON

7. PEPPER – _____ – _____ – TENSED

8. BISHOP – _____ – _____ – LARYNX

9. PEANUT – _____ – _____ – RIMMED

10. BLITHE – _____ – _____ – TERROR

Answers are on page 79.

Word Chains

11. TUNDRA – _____ – _____ – SEDATE

12. WIGWAM – _____ – _____ – MELTED

13. CARBON – _____ – _____ – TEDIUM

14. PURPLE – _____ – _____ – ORBITS

15. CATNAP – _____ – _____ – DERIVE

16. OUTPUT – _____ – _____ – SERAPH

17. RAISIN – _____ – _____ – UNDONE

18. OPERAS – _____ – _____ – PESTER

19. CARPET – _____ – _____ – LEDGER

20. FANJET – _____ – _____ – BERATE

Answers are on page 79.

Answers are on page 79.

MENSA SCORING	
Average Mensa Score:	55%

Consecutive Homophones

Homophones like "hair" and "hare" are common enough, but they rarely appear as consecutive words in the same sentence. Yet, it can happen, especially in sentences with proper names. For example, the sentence "Is it true that Jerry Herman got angry when a troupe of amateur actors proceeded to _____ _____?" can be completed with MAIM and MAME. Try to complete sensible sentences with consecutive homophones.

1. When Dennis gets a little too _____, _____ barks at him.

2. Has anyone from your _____ _____ through your office today?

3. Did the coach issue jersey number _____ _____ _____ many players?

4. He paid _____ _____ dinners.

5. All that _____ _____ be believed.

6. He gave the bishop two, the priest one, and the _____ _____.

7. Before you write down my _____, _____ until I empty my pockets.

8. The boat shop was featuring a _____ _____.

9. Will the soldier riding on the _____ _____ anybody?

10. Do many residents of _____ _____ through Vatican City?

Answers are on page 80.

Consecutive Homophones

11. How was _____ _____ to fool his brother?

12. When you buy virtual fishing software, you don't get a _____ _____.

13. Is it true that a musician who plays _____ _____ faster than one who plays brass?

14. He wore an Indonesian shirt with a _____ _____.

15. Does one's _____ _____ faster than one's toe?

16. The head of the _____ _____ open the zebra carcass.

17. In an updated version of the classical play, *Oedipus* _____ _____ his father's new car.

18. Would a pigeon that attempts a _____ _____ if it's successful?

19. Did he ever _____ _____ World?

20. Why would his favorite _____ _____ from the circus?

Answers are on page 80.

MENSA SCORING	
Average Mensa Score:	65%

Wisecrack Puzzles 8

Here we have wisecrack answers following riddle questions. Find the word in the blanks. Q: "Did you ever dream about being Tiger Woods's _____?" A: "No, but I once dreamed I was Arnold Palmer's Lincoln Continental." The word in the blank is CADDY.

1. Q: Mister, can you _____ a ten?
A: Only if I bowl cross-alley.

2. Q: Are you planning to give your wife a _____ this year?
A: Not if it means breaking up a flush.

3. Q: Where else could you have four _____ in Moscow?
A: At a Russian chess club.

4. Q: Did you hit _____ on the drive over here?
A: No, he's still in London waiting for the balloon to come down.

5. Q: How good are you at handling yourself on the _____?
A: Give me two pairs of abscissas and ordinates, and I'll calculate them for you any time.

6. Q: Where can I find papal _____?
A: I'm sorry, but the Pope doesn't own any livestock now.

7. Q: Does the lingerie department have _____ slips?
A: Probably not as many as the personnel department.

8. Q: Would you like to share some peanut butter and _____?
A: I can't, my guitar is in the repair shop.

9. Q: Have you found the _____ yet?
A: Yes, and it's 1 percent salt and 99 percent water.

10. Q: When can I expect a _____?
A: Eight hours after the plane leaves from Prague.

Answers are on page 80.

Wisecrack Puzzles

11. Q: When working at a grocery, were you ever a _____?
A: If I did, I'd have been a king if I made it to the last row.

12. Q: Can you show me a _____?
A: The square root of 3 divided by 2 if the angle is 60°.

13. Q: Is there a _____ in this mall?
A: The sporting goods store's archery department should have one.

14. Q: Have you ever eaten a vegetarian meal on a _____?
A: Yes, and I've eaten them on curved surfaces, too.

15. Q: What's the greatest number of _____ you've seen on a wedding cake?
A: About 1,000, when the groom didn't show up and the bride couldn't stop crying.

16. Q: Is steel the best _____?
A: He wasn't as good as Toscanini.

17. Q: Does this Stephen King story have a good _____?
A: Yes, and it's in the best part of the cemetery.

18. Q: Have you ever seen a black _____?
A: Yes, when the only auto anyone could buy was a Model T.

19. Q: Did your husband bring you _____ yesterday?
A: Yes. White, buckwheat, and cake, all sifted.

20. Q: Are there any _____ in the aviary?
A: No, you keep walking in the same direction.

Answers are on page 80.

MENSA SCORING	
Average Mensa Score:	65%

Bridge Words

Sometimes, a word or a name acts as a bridge between two other words or names by forming a common expression or title after the first and before the second. For example, a bridge word between JENNIFER and BERRY would be JUNIPER, making JENNIFER JUNIPER and JUNIPER BERRY. Try to find a bridge word connecting the following words.

1. SUNDAY and SQUARE

2. GREAT and PIE

3. OPEN and SEED

4. BROADWAY and LOUIS

5. SHAKESPEARE and BALL

6. MONKEY and ADMINISTRATION

7. PERPETUAL and SICKNESS

8. PLAIN and FUDGE

9. DIRTY and POTTER

10. UPPER and ACTION

Answers are on page 81.

Bridge Words

11. GRATEFUL and DUCK

12. CORN and CATCHER

13. BIG and CART

14. CHICKEN and WOMEN

15. FALLEN and HAIR

16. TAR and SPLIT

17. SNOW and KNIGHT

18. SKIN and PURPLE

19. JURY and BALLOON

20. DRAFT and BELLY

Answers are on page 81.

Answers are on page 81.

MENSA SCORING

Average Mensa Score:	70%

Tri-peaters

According to the laws of mathematics, there are 15,600 permutations (combinations where order counts) of three different letters. So, without some advance planning, it would be unlikely that a sentence would have consecutive words where the last three letters of the first word are the first three letters of the next. However, with some planning, it can happen. For example, the sentence "Many ba___ ___ngsters speak both English and French" makes sense with the three-letter combination YOU. The sentence becomes "Many bayou youngsters speak both English and French." Try to find the missing repeating three-letter combination, or "tri-peater," so that these sentences make sense (the tri-peater may or may not form a word):

1. It's hard to s___ ___ed people out of bed.

2. Is the matter of the high school building an___ ___t on the agenda?

3. The frivolous man s___ ___irely too much money to his favorite nephew.

4. A ball with too much l___ ___en misses the pocket.

5. Mighty Mo___ ___d to be my favorite comic book hero.

6. Some critics consider C3PO a rather bl ___ ___roid.

7. The pitcher never got to b___ ___il he was traded to a National League team.

8. Don Quixote went on a uni___ ___st.

9. A person needing a good bar___ ___ied on the local cooper.

10. If the water is polluted, one should not ba___ ___re.

Answers are on page 82.

Tri-peaters

11. The furniture store is selling so___ ___ter than it's selling love seats.

12. It's hard to h___ ___alism.

13. The secret ag___ ___ered the room.

14. Give the mer___ ___s of time to cool.

15. The cho___ ___hed through the piece.

16. Farmers don't need a special gar___ ___ense.

17. Some family members and the vi___ ___ried the casket.

18. Will he be the n___ ___remist to be caught?

19. Don't make the man in the Must___ ___ry.

20. Greetings f___ ___e.

Answers are on page 82.

MENSA SCORING

Average Mensa Score:	85%

Vanity Auto Messages

When *Rocky* was an extremely popular film, the occasional fan who drove a Toyota would remove some of the letters, leaving the message "YO." In the same spirit, a part-time teacher driving a Mitsubishi could remove letters leaving "SUB." In order to be aesthetically pleasing, the vanity auto message must be made with consecutive letters. Try to find the messages for the following people, who might be driving a Toyota, Mitsubishi, Plymouth, Chevrolet, Volkswagen, Saturn, or Explorer.

1. A burglar

2. A teller of ancient tales

3. An undertaker

4. An umpire

5. A poodle breeder

6. An actor

7. A political hack

8. A bullfighter

9. An HR compensation specialist

10. A greeter

Answers are on page 82.

MENSA SCORING

Average Mensa Score:	75%

Part II

SOMETHING IN COMMON

Answers are on pages 83–86.

Something in Common

Discover what all the things in Column A have in common that none of the things in Column B have in common. Here are two examples.

COLUMN A	COLUMN B
Glory	Practical
Sword	Yard
Marching	Drum
Coming	Patriotic
Grapes	Sit

All of the words in Column A are in "The Battle Hymn of the Republic."

COLUMN A	COLUMN B
Vacuum	Batter
Aardvark	Horror
Smooth	Inspired
Reed	Mangrove
Caboose	Deter

You'll find many correct ways to state a solution. For instance, in the second example, it's valid to say, "The words in Column A have the same vowel back-to-back." Consider your answer correct if it states the right idea in any reasonable way. We include Column B to help you eliminate answers that are technically correct, but trivial (such as words with less than fifteen letters).

We've arranged these puzzles in three sections: "Miscellany" (pages 29–35), "Same-Size Words" (pages 36–42), and "Names & Places" (pages 43–49). In addition, we've thrown in one bonus puzzle, "Crazy Q," at the end of this section. *Answers are on pages 83–86.*

Miscellany

Try to find what all the words in Column A and none of the words in Column B have in common.

1. COLUMN A | COLUMN B

COLUMN A	COLUMN B
Panacea	Oratorio
Alimony	Strengthening
Telepathy	Crumbs
Embryonic	Embryo
Panorama	Etymology

2.

COLUMN A	COLUMN B
Saw	Numb
Adage	Sodium
Faithful	Deny
Paint	Octagon
Hat	Also

3.

COLUMN A	COLUMN B
Tar	Cat
Gem	Ilk
Can	Feed
Corn	We
Go	Bump

Answers are on page 83.

SOMETHING IN COMMON

29

Miscellany

4. COLUMN A   COLUMN B

COLUMN A	COLUMN B
Blue	Mandolin
Mocking	Pinky
Bath	Refusal
Seed	Hymn
Humming	Iodine

5.

COLUMN A	COLUMN B
Pull	Cloud
Noodle	Place
Bug	Empire
Boner	Bridal
Hussy	Part

6.

COLUMN A	COLUMN B
Backgammon	Chess
Monopoly	Poker
Trivial Pursuit	Dominos
Parcheesi	Checkers
Craps	Roulette

Answers are on page 83.

Miscellany

7. COLUMN A   COLUMN B

COLUMN A	COLUMN B
Court	Break
War	Carpet
Rights	Uneventful
Service	Abstract
Unrest	Mourn

8. COLUMN A   COLUMN B

COLUMN A	COLUMN B
Software	Key
Garden	Wallet
Telephone	Lamp
Bed	Motion
Fruit	Digit

9. COLUMN A   COLUMN B

COLUMN A	COLUMN B
Football	Table tennis
Basketball	Soccer
Tennis	Lacrosse
Shuffleboard	Hockey
Horseshoes	Volleyball

Answers are on page 83.

SOMETHING IN COMMON

Miscellany

10. COLUMN A   COLUMN B
Devil   Deer
Hold   Dear
Quest   Pride
Witch   Knit
Tray   Early

11. COLUMN A   COLUMN B
Hundred   Pine
Fool   Hearing
Water   Melody
Child   Arrogant
Living   Crimson

12. COLUMN A   COLUMN B
Spitting   Slouching
Smoking   Walking flat-footed
Swearing   Banging doors
Nail biting   Squinting
Using excessive slang   Eavesdropping

Answers are on page 83.

Miscellany

13. COLUMN A   COLUMN B

COLUMN A	COLUMN B
Hand	Fill
Dollar	Cringe
Senate	Potato
Wild	Rifle
Unpaid	Interval

14. COLUMN A   COLUMN B

COLUMN A	COLUMN B
Political	Flop
Wild	During
Private	Lime
Tea	Tortilla
Exploration	Abutment

15. COLUMN A   COLUMN B

COLUMN A	COLUMN B
Master	Helm
Horse	Stiff
Back	Pearl
Mile	Oat
Note	Front

Answers are on page 84.

SOMETHING IN COMMON

Miscellany

16. COLUMN A
Lime
Spot
Moon
Day
Flash

COLUMN B
From
Gold
Spare
Pole
Mat

17. COLUMN A
Private
Beef
Rolling
Preferred
In

COLUMN B
Trill
Harmless
Thimble
Market
Purple

18. COLUMN A
Act
Are
Any
Lain
Lied

COLUMN B
Atom
Bat
Drum
Earn
Link

Answers are on page 84.

Miscellany

19. COLUMN A   COLUMN B

COLUMN A	COLUMN B
Short	Poultry
Permanent	Cosmetic
Heat	Copper
Sound	If
Radio	Shield

20.

COLUMN A	COLUMN B
Goose	Part
Man	Saw
Ball	Once
Flake	Luck
Cone	Cow

21.

COLUMN A	COLUMN B
Dander	Diamond
Dream	Dish
Dog	Dragon
Dope	Dwindle
Dare	Dogma

Answers are on page 84.

SOMETHING IN COMMON

MENSA SCORING

Average Mensa Score: 45%

Same-Size Words

What do all the words in Column A and none of the words in Column B have in common?

1. COLUMN A	COLUMN B
Curving	Tuneful
Unravel	Combine
Vaunted	Vulture
Outlive	Quality
Devious	Shaving

2. COLUMN A	COLUMN B
Ear	End
Eon	Elm
Eve	Eye
Eat	Eel
Ewe	Egg

3. COLUMN A	COLUMN B
Bar	Cow
Bag	Are
Box	Tar
Lot	Rim
Pit	Fig

Answers are on page 84.

Same-Size Words

4. COLUMN A   COLUMN B

Over   Pull
Star   Ache
Plan   Size
Flee   Idea
Firs   Hunt

5. COLUMN A   COLUMN B

Umpire   Module
Chorus   Chunky
Crusts   Doused
Pullet   Quotas
Butter   Uglier

6. COLUMN A   COLUMN B

Movie   Plant
Super   Break
Lucky   Lemon
North   Angle
First   Stole

Answers are on page 84.

SOMETHING IN COMMON

Same-Size Words

7. COLUMN A   COLUMN B

Junk	Peck
Carp	Seek
Cask	Tank
Mark	Work
Sock	Each

8. COLUMN A   COLUMN B

Steak	Apple
Baker	Skunk
Miles	Quake
Inure	Vodka
Trout	Agile

9. COLUMN A   COLUMN B

Each	Love
Ring	Like
Lame	Sing
Lack	Rule
Road	Ever

Answers are on page 84.

Same-Size Words

10. COLUMN A   COLUMN B

Emblem	Raider
Retire	Dented
Church	Stress
Edited	Proper
Deride	Errand

11. COLUMN A   COLUMN B

Haven	Beard
Drive	Clans
Hated	Grove
Raped	Ivory
Fared	Shunt

12. COLUMN A   COLUMN B

Impair	Aspire
Simply	Camper
Shrimp	Primes
Pimple	Crispy
Blimps	Noodle

Answers are on pages 84–85.

SOMETHING IN COMMON

Same-Size Words

13. COLUMN A   COLUMN B

Piano   Fetch
Graph   Peach
Coded   Rusty
Candy   Ample
Stool   Drake

14. COLUMN A   COLUMN B

Olive   Glove
Canoe   Forty
Pinto   Oasis
Groin   Igloo
Joust   Radon

15. COLUMN A   COLUMN B

Bear   Clam
Meat   Tack
Fair   Snow
Fish   Fuzz
Bull   Fare

Answers are on page 85.

Same-Size Words

16. COLUMN A

Pane	Plan
Noun	Earn
Long	Duck
Fits	Trip
Gram	Moth

COLUMN B

17. COLUMN A

Beat	Kill
Burn	Itch
Felt	Lamp
Ache	More
Less	Each

COLUMN B

18. COLUMN A

Hand	Oath
Fire	Soot
Drop	Bran
Ward	Pony
Ache	Sick

COLUMN B

Answers are on page 85.

SOMETHING IN COMMON

Same-Size Words

19. COLUMN A   COLUMN B

Rest	Rack
Back	Able
Dice	Stem
Bust	Gasp
Fled	Love

20. COLUMN A   COLUMN B

Worm	Nail
Ends	Salt
Text	Flee
Mark	Boil
Work	Also

21. COLUMN A   COLUMN B

Hare	Bone
Pool	Claw
Ills	Only
Kill	Glee
Tone	Life

Answers are on page 85.

MENSA SCORING

Average Mensa Score: 45%

Names & Places

Try to discover what all the names and places in Column A and none of the names and places in Column B have in common.

1. COLUMN A

"Nature Boy"
"Mona Lisa"
"Unforgettable"
"Christmas Song"
"Too Young"

COLUMN B

"All the Way"
"Misty"
"Harbor Lights"
"Chances Are"
"Lady of Spain"

2. COLUMN A

Eleanor
Maxwell
Desmond
Mary
Molly

COLUMN B

Teddy
Garth
Judy
Harriet
Karim

3. COLUMN A

Brown
Tufts
Brandeis
Yale
Radcliffe

COLUMN B

Duke
Georgetown
Baylor
Stanford
Columbia

Answers are on page 85.

SOMETHING IN COMMON

Names & Places

4. COLUMN A

Ernie Banks
Sid Luckman
Gale Sayers
Stan Mikita
Michael Jordan

COLUMN B

Y.A. Tittle
Wayne Gretzky
Mark Spitz
Yogi Berra
Karim Abdul Jabbar

5. COLUMN A

Blue Boy
Washington Crossing
  the Delaware
Strike Three
American Gothic
Whistler's Mother

COLUMN B

Mona Lisa
The Absynthe Drinkers

Sunday in the Park
Wheat Fields
Guernica

6. COLUMN A

Ravel
Debussy
Berlioz
Offenbach
Poulenc

COLUMN B

Vivaldi
Wagner
Copland
Haydn
Chopin

Answers are on page 85.

Names & Places

7. COLUMN A

Grover
Big Bird
Count the Count
Kermit
Miss Piggy

COLUMN B

Mickey Mouse
Daffy Duck
Woody Woodpecker
Snoopy
Tony the Tiger

8. COLUMN A

North by Northwest
Operation Petticoat
Charade
Philadelphia Story
To Catch a Thief

COLUMN B

Gone with the Wind
Casablanca
Gigi
A Hard Day's Night
Exodus

9. COLUMN A

Noah
Isaac
Cain
Sarah
Benjamin

COLUMN B

Aaron
Isaiah
Delilah
Jesus
Herod

Answers are on page 85.

SOMETHING IN COMMON

45

Names & Places

10. COLUMN A

Sweet Charity
Irma La Douce
Terms of Endearment
The Apartment
The Yellow Rolls Royce

COLUMN B

Raiders of the Lost Ark
My Fair Lady
Annie Hall
Casablanca
Invasion of the Body Snatchers

11. COLUMN A

Ulysses S. Grant
Robert E. Lee
Abraham Lincoln
Jefferson Davis
William Tecumseh
    Sherman

COLUMN B

George Washington
Franklin D. Roosevelt
Henry Ford
John Jay
John Glenn

12. COLUMN A

Lake Erie
Crater Lake
Lake Placid
Shasta Lake
Lake Superior

COLUMN B

Lake Geneva
Loch Lomond
Lake Winnipeg
Lake Titicaca
Lake Victoria

Answers are on pages 85–86.

Names & Places

13. COLUMN A   COLUMN B

Alaska	Oregon
Ohio	Maine
Idaho	Arkansas
Indiana	Kansas
Alabama	California

14. COLUMN A   COLUMN B

France	Spain
Austria	Poland
Germany	Belgium
Italy	Sweden
Switzerland	Norway

15. COLUMN A   COLUMN B

COLUMN A	COLUMN B
"Anything You Can Do"	"On the Street Where You Live"
"We Can Make Believe"	"Climb Every Mountain"
"Small World"	"Maria"
"People Will Say We're in Love"	"There Is Nothing Like a Dame"
"Do You Love Me?"	"If I Were a Rich Man"

Answers are on page 86.

Names & Places

16. COLUMN A

Buffalo, NY
Boise, ID
Los Angeles, CA
Richmond, VA
Topeka, KS

COLUMN B

Miami, FL
Palm Beach, FL
Denver, CO
Albany, NY
Seattle, WA

17. COLUMN A

Donald Duck
Woodstock
Roadrunner
Tweety
Heckyl

COLUMN B

Elmer Fudd
Snoopy
Pogo
Felix
Pluto

18. COLUMN A

Abraham
Peter
Lot
Jezebel
Barabbas

COLUMN B

Joseph
Isaac
Moses
Rachel
Paul

Answers are on page 86.

19. COLUMN A

Edgar
Donald
Franklin
Bertram
Samuel

COLUMN B

Albert
Frederick
Garth
Harold
Felix

20. COLUMN A

Dave
Joe
Jack
Tim
Bob

COLUMN B

Bert
Al
Fred
Mike
Larry

21. COLUMN A

French Roast
Java Mocha
Guatemala Antigua
Colombia Supremo
Jamaica Blue
Mountain

COLUMN B

Kentucky Bluegrass
Italian Ices
Canada Dry
Japanese Sandman
American Pie

Answers are on page 86.

SOMETHING IN COMMON

MENSA SCORING

Average Mensa Score: 45%

Crazy Q (Bonus)

These sentences all contain words with one or more Q's in them. Find words or names that make sense in the sentence. Here's an example: There were 25 Q _ _ _ _ _ _ _ _ _ _ on the English Q _ _ _ _. The missing words are QUESTIONS and QUIZ.

1. Sancho Panza was Don Q _ _ _ _ _ _ _ _'s _ Q _ _ _ _ _.

2. Zucchini is a high-Q _ _ _ _ _ _ _ _ _ Q _ _ _ _.

3. The football coach needed another
   Q _ _ _ _ _ _ _ _ _ _ _ _ on his _ Q _ _ _.

4. He told a duck to Q _ _ _ Q _ _ _ _ _ _ _ _.

5. _ _ _ Q _ _ _ _ stories are Q _ _ _ _ popular among superstitious people in the northwestern states.

6. The man standing near a _ _ _ Q _ _ in Cairo was holding a _ _ _ Q _ _ _ of flowers.

7. Our tour guide at the _ Q _ _ _ _ _ _ _ told us the difference between an octopus and a _ Q _ _ _.

8. The critics were Q _ _ _ _ to give bad reviews to the popular action movie's _ _ Q _ _ _.

9. She was _ _ _ Q _ _ _ _ _ _ _ _ _ from the contest for using a sewing machine to make some stitches on her Q _ _ _ _.

10. The adventurer managed to live through a 9.2 Richter Scale _ _ _ _ _ Q _ _ _ _ and a fall into a Q _ _ _ _ _ _ _ _ pit.

Answers are on page 86.

Part III

IN THE STORE

Answers are on pages 87–90.

Electronics Store

The sentence "The voters in the 1996 elections did not let Robert _____ President" can be completed with DOLBY (Dole be). Find a word or name associated with an electronics store that would make these sentences sensible.

1. Is that slowpoke _____ to leave on time?

2. That 'eadstrong 'ussy with red 'air would _____ mind on any topic.

3. Can the person who sold you a Big _____ you some Chicken McNuggets, too?

4. Can the seamstress _____ pads for football players?

5. The next time we go _____ go to a movie.

6. The minute the cook took the fried chicken out of the _____ boom was heard.

7. The next time you need a three-letter word for a pea covering, _____.

8. Mr. Cooke's fans loved all the songs that _____.

9. Wherever he _____ rain kept falling on his seat.

10. Mrs. Park keeps hoping that _____ win every game he pitches.

Answers are on page 87.

Electronics Store

11. The plastic surgeon had to _____ and cheeks with tissue.

12. Outfielders tend to _____ farther when power hitters are at bat.

13. He took a slice of _____ of corn, and a piece of chicken.

14. If your opponent tries to lower the _____ him with speed.

15. Yes _____ tables are perfect for conferences.

16. The gift-wrapping department is short of _____.

17. No other actress who played Sally Bowles was able to _____ Minneli.

18. Temperamental people get _____ the pettiest things.

19. If the department _____ me, please tell him I'll call back within five minutes.

20. Is it true that whenever Crusoe went for a _____ Friday accompanied him?

Answers are on page 87.

Answers are on page 87.

MENSA SCORING	
Average Mensa Score:	40%

Home Improvement Store 2

The sentence "The Mantle fan once saw the _____ hot dog at Yankee Stadium" can be completed with MAKITA (Mick eat a). Find a word or name associated with a home improvement store that would make the sentences sensible.

1. Do people who live near San Francisco _____ often between visits to church?

2. Shelley _____ little action when she filled in for Farrah Fawcett in "Charlie's Angels."

3. Don't _____ , or you'll wake 'er up.

4. Bill C's veep was _____.

5. A father's praise will often make a daughter or _____ with delight.

6. The _____ Mustang was parked next to his royal Rolls Royce.

7. After the sudden _____ of cards were flying off the pool chairs.

8. Hat ownership in Scotland runs about one _____ person.

9. Once again, the gambler came _____ of cash.

10. You must sign the _____ it won't be valid.

Answers are on page 88.

11. A test that's too _____ cause many students to fail the course.

12. When a trend intensifies, it's difficult to _____.

13. When the letters are shown by _____ is the consonant most often picked.

14. People used to say "_____ to me" during the sixties.

15. _____ alcohol be more profitable to make than brandy?

16. Lifting weights can make your _____.

17. Since we're short of bacon, allot only one _____ breakfast.

18. The cabin can be heated with either _____ wood.

19. The trustful child with the new _____ me hold it.

20. The worker with greater _____ his salary increase twice as much.

Answers are on page 88.

IN THE STORE

MENSA SCORING

Average Mensa Score:	30%

Pet Store

The sentence "Add the _____ the egg mixture, cook, and you have a Denver omelet" can be completed with HAMSTER (ham, stir). Find a word or name associated with a pet store so that each sentence makes sense.

1. Would my dinner _____ five dollars more if I order a dessert?

2. If you leave _____ in the ignition, somebody will probably steal it.

3. If you want to catch a trout or a _____ is necessary to buy some fishing supplies.

4. How _____ Pennsylvania be so far from Philadelphia?

5. How can people who swim in the _____ from others when they exit the pool?

6. _____ help Barbie study for her next science test.

7. Is the Speaker of the _____ bread with the Senate Whip?

8. His hole card is a nine of _____.

9. This boat requires an _____ good rower.

10. When you contemplate a long time _____ often go from cradle to grave.

Answers are on page 88.

Pet Store

11. They offer chocolate _____ and coffees.

12. When an employee is very _____ increases are often earned.

13. When it comes to creamy desserts, I can _____ up in no time.

14. I gave my sales _____ and linoleum samples.

15. Can the trained _____ the way to the walrus pool?

16. The ship will lose its _____ the wind gets any worse.

17. Can the song be changed _____ Malone doesn't die?

18. Does your _____ crochet when she's home in the evening?

19. He found Winnie the _____ and Eeyore even less interesting.

20. He first climbed to the top of the mountain's highest _____ in the seventies.

Answers are on page 88.

Answers are on page 88.

IN THE STORE

MENSA SCORING

Average Mensa Score:	30%

Toy Store

The sentence "Two of the risks incurred by playing football would ____ and back injuries" can be completed with BEANIE (be knee). Find a word or name associated with a toy store that would make each of these sentences sensible.

1. Would a salad ____ a good thing to have in this restaurant?

2. You may select Doublemint, Trident, or Big Red when you're ready to ____.

3. Does the CIA teach some of its agents to ____ control techniques?

4. If Rocky Balboa repeated words, he'd probably say ____.

5. When a seal is a ____ is still very young.

6. Dad ____ and Sis on an allowance of three dollars a week each.

7. This cat will chase a ____ he catches it.

8. How far can a ____ from the beach?

9. His insurance plan can ____ surgery if it's judged unnecessary.

10. When they took the subway or the ____ Larry, and Curly would practice their routines.

Answers are on page 89.

11. When the kids put on a _____ administrators encourage the parents to attend.

12. Mechanics _____ cylinders as important components of the braking system.

13. If you throw a _____ can hurt someone.

14. An outdoor cat is liable to _____ all kinds of rubbish.

15. For many firms, 2001 was a _____ for profitability.

16. I had to let the chicken _____, but I did get a thigh.

17. Will you let the girl with her hand on her _____ for the picture?

18. The shipper had to _____ drivers when the price of gas was high.

19. Can the people who are out on that _____ the coastline?

20. Some writers like to make _____ and hope the readers can figure out what they mean.

Answers are on page 89.

MENSA SCORING

Average Mensa Score:	30%

Music Store

The sentence "I am going _____ my suitcase" can be completed with TUPAC (to pack). Fill in the blank with a word or a name associated with a music store.

1. If it can happen to me, it can happen to _____.

2. Making a charitable contribution near the end of the _____ be a smart tax-saving move.

3. Did Phillip _____ many records for tobacco sales?

4. Does a Holiday _____ have a single faucet or a double faucet?

5. When he was seen reading the latest issue of _____ bus, he said, "What, me worry?"

6. She saw Rock Hudson and Sandra _____ a cable TV movie station.

7. After you shine it, you should _____.

8. Many cooks put a little fresh _____ Swedish meatballs.

9. For many people, Good Friday is a _____.

10. He handed the _____ offer for the house, and the seller rejected it.

Answers are on page 89.

11. "You have a lot of _____ might have said to the King of Siam.

12. We have gallons of _____ of paper, and tons of flour and sugar.

13. The school has a _____ and field program.

14. Our father took the trouble to _____, so we are his children.

15. In Laker lore, the early 2000s will be known as the Kobe and _____.

16. She had a minor speaking _____ the play.

17. Tomatoes on the _____ taste better than those that were picked days ago.

18. The _____ on a 5-year CD is usually higher than on a 1-year CD.

19. In Colorado _____ magazines sell as well per capita as in Denver.

20. The mastery of _____ necessary to become a successful engineer.

Answers are on page 89.

IN THE STORE

MENSA SCORING

Average Mensa Score:	35%

Bookstore

The sentence "If Mister T changed his name to Edward, would people call him _____?" can be completed with MYSTERY (Mister E). Find a word or name associated with a book and magazine store to complete each sentence.

1. During the Vietnam War, some villages were completely _____ an hour or two.

2. This Easter, when you prepare the _____ it cook thoroughly.

3. The plastic surgeon was preparing _____, cheek, and nose procedures.

4. Will the makers of Orange _____ an increase in market share?

5. Wherever I _____ follow me and get into my food.

6. Sometimes, a _____ into a duck when they both go after a breadcrumb.

7. It is rumored that there is a lot of _____ city government.

8. If _____ a crime, it is my duty to report it.

9. I prefer to play _____ the morning and golf in the afternoon.

10. Too many actors tend to _____ up when they recite their lines.

Answers are on page 90.

Bookstore

11. Do people with a large _____ their relatives more often?

12. Is picking up one's _____ for lazy people?

13. You have a choice of pork, _____ beef.

14. Betty Ford once remarked that a sweater _____ better than a suit.

15. The suit looked terrible on Capone, but it _____ very well.

16. They put their tour of the Liberty _____ on their list of must-see attractions.

17. It is rumored that Al _____ try to run for president again one day.

18. Some friends gave Edgar Allen _____ to trim for Christmas.

19. It is hard _____ through brackish waters.

20. First you hard-boil the Easter egg, then you _____.

Answers are on page 90.

IN THE STORE

MENSA SCORING

Average Mensa Score: 30%

Gift Buying

Visiting so many stores in these puzzle sections can easily inspire thoughts about buying truly appropriate gifts. Here are two examples of such gifts: a grill for someone who conducts interrogations or a suit for a person who works in a law office.

Find a truly appropriate gift for a person who:

1. Eats fast

2. Reviews bad movies

3. Paints houses

4. Makes close friendships

5. Neither wins nor loses

6. Is short of breath

7. Likes to phone people

8. Stands guard

9. Gets computers to start

10. Likes to make reservations

Answers are on page 90.

MENSA SCORING

Average Mensa Score: 70%

Part IV

Hidden Places

Answers are on pages 91–93.

Countries

Sometimes, the name of a country is hiding in the consecutive letters within a sentence. For example, FRANCE is hiding in, "The runners who lived at the top of the cliff ran centuries ago" (clifF RAN CEnturies). Find the name of a country hiding in the consecutive letters within these sentences.

1. You all must pay it back, or each of you will be in trouble.

2. Was Doctor Doolittle's favorite animal a glib yak?

3. A true optimist will never let hope rush away.

4. How often can a daydream come true?

5. Is there a health spa in this hotel?

6. They are going in diametrically opposite directions.

7. Is the county fair a nice place to visit?

8. The foot with which I lead is my left one.

9. He owns a ranch in Arizona.

10. The foods we deny ourselves are usually tasty.

Answers are on page 91.

Countries

11. I put it on Gary's credit card.

12. I can't stand this truss I am wearing.

13. Nineteen sixty-four was a vital year in the civil rights movement.

14. A lack of oxygen is a major danger at very high altitudes.

15. He gave Caleb a nonrefundable deposit.

16. Making a foolish decision can anger many people.

17. Where can one watch a decent play for less than ten dollars?

18. Every animal in the zoo is fed the proper amount of food.

19. The barber gave my hair a quick trim.

20. Both Topol and Zero Mostel starred in *Fiddler on the Roof.*

Answers are on page 91.

HIDDEN PLACES

MENSA SCORING	
Average Mensa Score:	90%

North American Cities

On occasion, you'll find the name of a North American city (United States, Canada, or Mexico) hidden in the consecutive letters within a sentence. For example, "The tennis player had trouble adjusting from a hard surface to a gravelly surface" is hiding OMAHA (frOM A HArd). Find the name of a North American city in the consecutive letters within these sentences.

1. According to history books, the *Clermont* really did run on steam.

2. If the book were to receive a final ban, you wouldn't find it in the library.

3. The politician thought he could coax academics into endorsing him.

4. How much money do I owe the tax collector?

5. When I play in a combo, I seldom have time to study.

6. The Huskies are playing the Lobos tonight.

7. He won a gold medal last year and a silver medal the year before.

8. He met with the senator on top-secret matters.

9. She ate toast and butter for breakfast.

10. The squeamish censor wanted to ban gory movies.

Answers are on page 92.

North American Cities

11. We were not deceived by his trickery.

12. Do you know how far gold prices have increased during the past twenty years?

13. Is the Big Mac on the list of North America's top ten fast foods?

14. If I were a successful farmer, I'd allocate ten percent of my crops to the poor.

15. Some liquids can harden very quickly.

16. The vassal emerged victorious.

17. When I eat salami, am I doing myself harm?

18. He claimed he once showed Mel Ott a way to improve his hitting.

19. Does the pier reach at least a hundred yards past the shoreline?

20. The investor was looking for land on Main Street.

Answers are on page 92.

HIDDEN PLACES

MENSA SCORING	
Average Mensa Score:	80%

European & Asian Cities 3

The name of a well-known European or Asian city may be buried in the consecutive letters in a sentence. For example, you'll find "I need a commitment from everyone at this meeting" is concealing ROME (fROM Everyone). Find the name of a European or Asian city buried in the consecutive letters within these sentences.

1. He loved to pin the tail on donkeys at birthday parties.

2. If you like Bartok, you'll love Dvorak.

3. In a game of golf, shooting two over par is called a double bogey.

4. Success in math ensures a wider choice of careers.

5. There was a mad rider on the bus.

6. Will Douglas go wild when he hears the news?

7. He has the talisman I lack.

8. Is it good luck to rub a Lincoln penny?

9. The next time you eat a great steak, remember to thank a rancher.

10. Shortening is thicker than oil.

Answers are on page 93.

European & Asian Cities

11. I am going to slow down when I get older.

12. He had never seen a paler movie star in his life.

13. After I ate nine hot dogs at the county fair, I gained two pounds.

14. The number lines ranged from negative ten to positive ten.

15. Madame LaPorte named her sons Emil and Pierre.

16. His hobbies were drag racing and ski jumping.

17. In my opinion, that gal is bonkers.

18. Did Eugene validate the data?

19. A new crop is about to be harvested.

20. The model hid her anorexia very well.

Answers are on page 93.

HIDDEN PLACES

MENSA SCORING	
Average Mensa Score:	80%

Bonus

NAME GAMES

Answers are on pages 94.

Names

Some people's first names and their homonyms can be used as words. For instance, the sentence "Tom couldn't tell if he was eating a tom or a hen turkey" uses both the name and its homonym. On the other hand, "Phil tried to fill the swimming pool with water" uses both a name and its homophone (a word that is not spelled the same but is pronounced the same). Fill in the blanks with names and their homonyms or homophones to create good, sensible sentences.

1. _____ was really good on the parallel bars and other _____ apparatus.

2. _____ _____ a hole in the back yard.

3. _____ used a _____ to help his father fix a flat tire.

4. _____ knew that "Z" is the _____ of Zorro.

5. _____ was strong enough to _____ a twenty-pound bucket of cement.

6. _____ read a story where the hero saves someone in the _____ of time.

7. _____ is the tallest _____ in his class.

8. _____ had to _____ because the water was too shallow for swimming.

9. _____ has been through hurricanes, tornadoes, and _____ force winds.

10. _____ _____ have to work late tomorrow.

MENSA SCORING	*Answers are on page 94.*
Average Mensa Score:	90%

Presidents

The names of United States Presidents are hidden in consecutive letters within each sentence below. Find the Presidents.

1. The gallant knight rescued a damsel in distress.

2. When Uncle Greg ran to answer the doorbell, he fell on his elbow.

3. In this fowl costume, I can't tell if you are a gander or a mallard.

4. There is no happier cetacean than one that avoids human contact.

5. I didn't know if he'd call my bluff or drop out.

6. Thirty years of heavy smoking made Cousin Oscar terminally ill.

7. The Gilberts moved back East after living in California for twelve years.

8. Columbus hoped that his crew would survive the hardships of the voyage.

9. He served the diplomat rum and Coca-Cola.

10. Are you the person who overcharged me for these shoes?

Answers are on page 94.

ANSWERS

*Some puzzles may have alternative solutions that we didn't
think of. Evaluate your results accordingly.*

Part I

Quick Word Puzzles

ANSWERS

Movies—2000 & Beyond

1. *Erin Brockovich*
2. *Pearl Harbor*
3. *Remember the Titans*
4. *Hannibal*
5. *Heist*
6. *Finding Forrester*
7. *Domestic Disturbance*
8. *Serendipity*
9. *Gladiator*
10. *Zoolander*

Puzzles on page 8

Movies—2000 & Beyond

11. *What Women Want*
12. *Training Day*
13. *Hearts in Atlantis*
14. *Miss Congeniality*
15. *Black Knight*
16. *Reindeer Games*
17. *Shrek*
18. *Hardball*
19. *Crouching Tiger, Hidden Dragon*
20. *Almost Famous*

Puzzles on page 9

Movies — the 1990s 2

1. *Rush Hour*
2. *Death Becomes Her*
3. *The Hurricane*
4. *Being John Malkovich*
5. *Pretty Woman*
6. *Analyze This*
7. *Hoop Dreams*
8. *Armageddon*
9. *Runaway Bride*
10. *Philadelphia*

Puzzles on page 10

Movies — the 1990s 2

11. *Sling Blade*
12. *Double Jeopardy*
13. *Fargo*
14. *Galaxy Quest*
15. *Pulp Fiction*
16. *True Lies*
17. *Three Kings*
18. *Jerry Maguire*
19. *Happy Gilmore*
20. *The Usual Suspects*

Puzzles on page 11

Half-Eaten Foods 3

1. ASPARAGUS
2. TORTILLA
3. PORTERHOUSE
4. HONEYDEW
5. GRAPEFRUIT
6. SAUERKRAUT
7. CASSEROLE
8. ZABAGLIONE
9. STRAWBERRY
10. FRANKFURTER

Puzzles on page 12

Half-Eaten Foods 3

11. CHOCOLATE
12. HASENPFEFFER
13. TEMPURA
14. ORANGE
15. KUMQUAT
16. HERRING
17. WATERMELON
18. BURRITO
19. ESCARGOT
20. DOUGHNUT

Puzzles on page 12

Half-Eaten Occupations 4

1. WRESTLER
2. STATISTICIAN
3. CHIROPRACTOR
4. HABERDASHER
5. VIOLINIST
6. METEOROLOGIST
7. ENTREPRENEUR
8. LANDLORD
9. PROFESSOR
10. PRESIDENT

Puzzles on page 13

Half-Eaten Occupations 4

11. COMPTROLLER
12. ACTUARY
13. THESPIAN
14. CONSULTANT
15. PSYCHOLOGIST
16. PHILANTHROPIST
17. PHOTOGRAPHER
18. TAXIDERMIST
19. MINISTER
20. SOLDIER

Puzzles on page 13

A-Team Puzzles 5

1. a way and away
2. atone and a tone
3. atrophy and a trophy
4. ado and a do
5. a venue and Avenue
6. alit and a lit *or* alighted and a lighted
7. a bet and abet
8. around and a round
9. abase and a base
10. a toll and atoll

Puzzles on page 14

A-Team Puzzles 5

11. aside and a side
12. a scent and ascent
13. asteroid and a steroid
14. A voided and avoided
15. a corn and acorn
16. a go and ago
17. a long and along
18. amuse and a muse
19. arose and a rose
20. a ward and award

Puzzles on page 15

1. CUTLET – LETTER – TERMED – MEDIAN
2. MADCAP – CAPPER – PERIOD – IODINE
3. SORBET – BETTOR – TORQUE – QUEUES
4. GRAHAM – HAMPER – PEROXY – OXYGEN
5. GROUSE – USEFUL – FULCRA – CRAFTY
6. MUSCAT – CATSUP – SUPPER – PERSON *OR*
   MUSCAT – CATNAP – NAPPER – PERSON
7. PEPPER – PERMIT – MITTEN – TENSED
8. BISHOP – HOPPED – PEDLAR – LARYNX
9. PEANUT – NUTMEG – MEGRIM – RIMMED
10. BLITHE – THESIS – SISTER – TERROR
11. TUNDRA – DRAMAS – MASSED – SEDATE
12. WIGWAM – WAMPUM – PUMMEL – MELTED
13. CARBON – BONNET – NETTED – TEDIUM
14. PURPLE – PLEADS – ADSORB – ORBITS
15. CATNAP – NAPKIN – KINDER – DERIVE
16. OUTPUT – PUTTER – TERSER – SERAPH
17. RAISIN – SINGER – GERUND – UNDONE
18. OPERAS – RASHER – HERPES – PESTER
19. CARPET – PETROL – ROLLED – LEDGER
20. FANJET – JETSOM – SOMBER – BERATE

Puzzles on page 16–17

Consecutive Homophones

1. rough and Ruff
2. past and passed
3. two, to, and too
4. for and four
5. cant and can't *or* Kant and cant
6. nun and none
7. weight and wait
8. sail and sale
9. sleigh and slay, *or* chute and shoot, *or* grille and grill
10. Rome and roam

Puzzles on page 18

Consecutive Homophones

11. Abel and able
12. real and reel
13. reeds and reads
14. Thai and tie
15. heel and heal
16. pride and pried *or* tour and tore
17. *Rex* and wrecks
18. coup and coo
19. see and Sea
20. flea and flee

Puzzles on page 19

Wisecrack Puzzles

1. spare
2. diamond
3. nights
4. fog
5. slopes
6. bulls
7. pink
8. jam
9. solution
10. check

Puzzles on page 20

Wisecrack Puzzles

11. checker
12. sign
13. Target
14. plane
15. tiers
16. conductor
17. plot
18. carnation
19. flowers
20. terns

Puzzles on page 21

Bridge Words 9

1. TIMES
2. PUMPKIN *or*
   AMERICAN
3. SESAME *or* TOURNA-
   MENT *or* TOP
4. JOE
5. PLAY
6. BUSINESS
7. MOTION
8. VANILLA *or*
   CHOCOLATE
9. HARRY
10. CLASS *or* COURT

Puzzles on page 22

Bridge Words 9

11. DEAD
12. DOG
13. APPLE, *or* PUSH,
    or OX
14. LITTLE
15. ANGEL
16. BABY
17. WHITE
18. DEEP *or* COLOR
19. TRIAL
20. BEER

Puzzles on page 23

Tri-peaters 10

1. stir and tired
2. annex and next
3. sent and entirely
4. loft and often
5. Mouse and used
6. bland and android
7. bunt and until
8. unique and quest
9. barrel and relied
10. bathe and there

Puzzles on page 24

Tri-peaters 10

11. sofas and faster
12. hide and idealism
13. agent and entered
14. merlot and lots
15. chorus and rushed
16. garlic and license
17. vicar and carried
18. next and extremist
19. Mustang and angry
20. from and Rome

Puzzles on page 25

81

1. SWAG (from Volkswagen)
2. LORE (from Explorer)
3. URN (from Saturn)
4. OUT (from Plymouth)
5. TOY (from Toyota) *or* WAG (from Volkswagen)
6. ROLE (from Chevrolet)
7. WAG (from Volkswagen) *or* MOUTH (from Plymouth)
8. OLE (from Chevrolet)
9. WAGE (from Volkswagen)
10. HI (from Mitsubishi) *or* YO (from Toyota)

Puzzles on page 26

Part II

Something in Common

ANSWERS

Miscellany

1. All have exactly four syllables.
2. All can be preceded by *old.*
3. All are words buried in a zodiac sign.
4. All form an expression with *bird.*
5. All form a dog breed by changing one letter (pull to puli, noodle to poodle, bug to pug, boner to boxer, and hussy to husky).
6. All are games that use dice.
7. All form an expression when preceded by *civil.*
8. All can contain a bug.
9. All can produce scoring plays of more than one point.
10. All can be preceded by *be* to form a word.

Puzzles on pages 29–32

Miscellany

11. All can be followed by *proof* to form a word or expression.

12. All are bad habits that involve the use of the mouth.

13. All can be followed by *bill* or *Bill* to form a word or expression.

14. All can be followed by *party* to form an expression.

15. All can be preceded by *quarter* to form a word or expression.

16. All can be followed by *light* to form a word or expression.

17. All can be followed by *stock* to form an expression.

18. All can be preceded by *comp* to form a word.

19. All can be followed by *wave* to form an expression.

20. All can be preceded by *snow* to form a word or expression.

21. All the *d*'s can be replaced by *t*'s to form a word.

Puzzles on page 32–35

Same-Size Words

1. All have exactly one *u* and one *v*.

2. All form a new word if the *e* is moved to the end.

3. All can be preceded by *sand* to form a word or expression.

4. All can be followed by *t* to form a word.

5. All can form a word by changing *u* to *e*.

6. All can be followed by *star* to form an expression.

7. All can be followed by *et* to form a word.

8. All can be anagrammed into one or more common words (takes, break, smile, urine, tutor).

9. All can be preceded by *b* to form a word.

10. All begin and end with the same two letters.

Puzzles on pages 32–39

11. All can add an *e* as the second letter to form a word.

12. All have *imp* within the word.

13. All can form a word or expression by adding *bar.*

14. All form a new word if the *o* is removed.

15. All can be followed by *market* to form an expression.

16. All form a word with the addition of *pro.*

17. All can be preceded by *heart* to form a word or expression.

18. All can be preceded by *back* to form a word.

19. All contain three letters that are consecutive in the alphabet (REST has R-S-T, etc.).

20. All form a word with *book.*

21. All can be preceded by *s* to form a word.

Puzzles on page 39–42

Puzzles on page 39–42

Names & Places   **3**

1. All are songs made famous by Nat King Cole.

2. All are names that appear in songs by the Beatles.

3. All are universities in New England.

4. All are athletes who played for Chicago teams.

5. All are paintings by English-speaking artists.

6. All are French composers.

7. All are Muppets characters.

8. All are movies starring Cary Grant.

9. All are biblical characters in Genesis.

10. All are movies starring Shirley MacLain.

Puzzles on page 43–46

Names & Places

11. All are people who played an active part in the Civil War.

12. All are lakes located fully or partially in the United States.

13. All are states whose names begin and end with a vowel.

14. All are countries that contain a portion of the Alps.

15. All are songs typically performed as a duet.

16. All the cities contain the same number of letters as their states.

17. All are bird cartoon characters.

18. All are biblical characters with only one vowel in their names (which may repeat).

19. All the names form common nicknames by dropping the last three letters.

20. All form a new word if the first letter is replaced with an *R*.

21. All are types of coffee.

Puzzles on page 46–49

Crazy Q (Bonus)

1. QUIXOTE and SQUIRE

2. QUALITY and SQUASH

3. QUARTERBACK and SQUAD

4. QUIT and QUACKING

5. SASQUASH and QUITE

6. MOSQUE and BOUQUET

7. AQUARIUM and SQUID

8. QUICK and SEQUEL

9. DISQUALIFIED and QUILT

10. EARTHQUAKE and QUICKSAND

Puzzles on page 50

Part III

In the Store

ANSWERS

Electronics Store · 1

1. Eveready (ever ready)
2. speaker (speak 'er)
3. Maxell (Mac sell)
4. Sony (sew knee)
5. outlets (out, let's)
6. Panasonic (pan, a sonic)
7. tripod (try "pod")
8. Samsung (Sam sung)
9. satellite (sat, a light)
10. channel (Chan'll)

Puzzles on page 52

Electronics Store · 1

11. Philips (fill lips)
12. playback (play back), *or* backup (back up), *or* stand
13. Pioneer (pie, an ear)
14. boombox (boom, box)
15. surround (sir, round)
16. Bose (bows) *or* tape
17. equalizer (equal Liza)
18. crossover (cross over)
19. headphones (head phones)
20. Walkman (walk, Man)

Puzzles on page 53

Home Improvement Store [2]

1. basin (Bay sin)
2. hacksaw (Hack saw)
3. poker (poke 'er) *or* router (rout 'er)
4. algae (Al G)
5. Sunbeam (son beam)
6. Kingsford (king's Ford) *or* planer (plainer)
7. Windex (wind, decks)
8. tamper (tam per)
9. Homelite (home light)
10. contractor (contract, or)

Puzzles on page 54

Home Improvement Store [2]

11. hardwood (hard would)
12. bucket (buck it), *or* stopper (stop 'er), *or* breaker (break 'er)
13. vanity (Vanna, T)
14. socket (sock it)
15. Woodgrain (Would grain), *or* Wood, *or* Can
16. Armstrong (arm strong)
17. stripper (strip per)
18. Kohler (coal or) *or* oiler (oil or)
19. toilet (toy let)
20. Skillsaw (skill saw)

Puzzles on page 55

Pet Store [3]

1. tabby (tab be)
2. Yorkie (your key)
3. basset (bass, it)
4. canary (can Erie,)
5. rawhide (raw hide)
6. Kennel (Ken'll)
7. housebreaking (House breaking)
8. Hartz (hearts)
9. Oranda (oar and a)
10. spaniel (span, you'll)

Puzzles on page 56

Pet Store [3]

11. Maltese (malt, teas,) *or* turtles
12. Shar-pei (sharp, pay)
13. whippet (whip it)
14. reptile (rep tile)
15. sealpoint (seal point)
16. mastiff (mast if)
17. Somali (so Molly)
18. monitor (ma knit or) *or* ant (aunt)
19. poodle (Pooh dull)
20. ridgeback (ridge back) *or* 'peke (peak)

Puzzles on page 57

Toy Store 4

1. Barbie (bar be)
2. Pikachu (pick a chew)
3. Mastermind (master mind)
4. yo-yo ("Yo, yo")
5. puppet (pup it)
6. Hasbro (has Bro)
7. rattle (rat 'til)
8. Shelby (shell be), or Barbie (bar be), or baby (bay be)
9. Barney (bar knee)
10. Elmo (el, Moe,)

Puzzles on page 58

Toy Store 4

11. Playskool (play, school)
12. Viewmaster (view master)
13. rocket (rock it)
14. dragon (drag in)
15. Lightyear (light year)
16. Lego (leg go) or Wingo (wing go)
17. hippos (hip pose)
18. firetruck (fire truck)
19. Yahtzee (yacht see)
20. Upwords (up words)

Puzzles on page 59

Music Store 5

1. U2 (you, too)
2. Yearwood (year would)
3. Morrisette (Morris set)
4. 'N Sync (Inn sink)
5. Madonna (*Mad* on a)
6. Dion (Dee on)
7. Buffett (buff it)
8. Dylan (dill in)
9. Sade (sad day) or Holiday (holiday)
10. Manilow (man a low)

Puzzles on page 60

Music Store 5

11. Nirvana (nerve," Anna)
12. Supremes (soup, reams)
13. soundtrack (sound track)
14. Cyrus (sire us)
15. Shakira (Shaq era)
16. Parton (part in)
17. vinyl (vine'll) or Plant (plant)
18. Raitt (rate)
19. Springsteen (Springs, teen)
20. Mathis (math is)

Puzzles on page 61

IN THE STORE ANSWERS

89

Bookstore

1. Sheldon (shelled in)
2. Hamlet (ham, let)
3. *Fortune* (for chin)
4. fantasy (Fanta see)
5. romance (roam, ants)
6. *Goosebumps* (goose bumps)
7. Grafton (graft in)
8. eyewitness (I witness)
9. Tennyson (tennis in)
10. Hammett (ham it)

Puzzles on page 62

Bookstore

11. Clancy (clan see)
12. literature (litter a chore)
13. L'Amour (lamb, or) *or* Fisher (fish, or)
14. Fitzgerald (fits Gerald)
15. fitness (fit Ness)
16. Bellow (Bell low)
17. gourmet (Gore may)
18. poetry (Poe a tree)
19. Turow (to row)
20. diet (dye it)

Puzzles on page 63

Gift Buying 7

1. *Eats fast* – scarf
2. *Reviews bad movies* – pan
3. *Paints houses* – coat
4. *Makes close friendships* – bond or tie
5. *Neither wins nor loses* – tie
6. *Is short of breath* – pants
7. *Likes to phone people* – ring
8. *Stands guard* – watch
9. *Gets computers to start* – boots
10. *Likes to make reservations* – book

Puzzles on page 64

Part IV

Hidden Places

ANSWERS

Countries   **1**

1. Korea (bacK OR EAch)
2. Libya (gLIB YAk)
3. Peru (hoPE RUsh)
4. Canada (CAN A DAydream)
5. Spain (SPA IN)
6. India (IN DIAmetrically)
7. Iran (faIR A Nice)
8. Chile (whiCH I LEad)
9. China (ranCH IN Arizona)
10. Sweden (foodS WE DENy)

Puzzles on page 66

Countries   **1**

11. Tonga (iT ON GAry's)
12. Russia (tRUSS I Am)
13. Italy (vITAL Year)
14. Jordan (maJOR DANger)
15. Lebanon (CaLEB A NON-refundable)
16. German (anGER MANY)
17. Chad (watCH A Decent)
18. Mali (aniMAL In)
19. Iraq (haIR A Quick)
20. Poland (ToPOL AND)

Puzzles on page 67

1. Montreal (ClerMONT REALly)
2. Albany (finAL BAN, You)
3. Oaxaca (cOAX ACAdemics)
4. Taxco (TAX COllector)
5. Boise (comBO, I SEldom)
6. Boston (LoBOS TONight)
7. Dallas (meDAL LASt)
8. Toronto (senaTOR ON TOp-)
9. Butte (BUTTEr)
10. Bangor (BAN GORy)

Puzzles on page 68

11. Reno (weRE NOt)
12. Fargo (FAR GOld)
13. Macon (MAC ON)
14. Merida (farMER, I'D Allocate)
15. Denver (harDEN VERy)
16. Salem (vassSAL EMerged)
17. Miami (salaMI, AM I)
18. Ottawa (OTT A WAy)
19. Pierre (PIER REach)
20. Olando (fOR LAND On)

Puzzles on page 69

European & Asian Cities

1. London (taiL ON DONkeys)
2. Tokyo (BarTOK, YOu'll)
3. Paris (PAR IS)
4. Athens (mATH ENSures)
5. Madrid (MAD RIDer)
6. Glasgow (DouGLAS GO Wild)
7. Manila (talisMAN I LAck)
8. Bali (ruB A LIncoln)
9. Ankara (thANK A RAncher)
10. Hanoi (tHAN OIl)

Puzzles on page 70

European & Asian Cities

11. Oslo (tO SLOw)
12. Palermo (PALER MOvie)
13. Riga (faiR, I GAined)
14. Berlin (numBER LINes)
15. Milan (EMIL ANd)
16. Agra (drAG RAcing)
17. Lisbon (gaL IS BONkers)
18. Geneva (EuGENE VAlidate)
19. Pisa (croP IS About)
20. Delhi (moDEL HId)

Puzzles on page 71

HIDDEN PLACES ANSWERS

Bonus

Name Games

ANSWERS

Names ∎1

1. Jim and gym
2. Doug and dug
3. Jack and jack
4. Mark *or* Marc and mark
5. Carrie and carry
6. Nick and nick
7. Guy and guy
8. Wade and wade
9. Gail and gale
10. May and may

Puzzles on page 73.

Presidents ∎2

1. ADAMS (a damsel)
2. GRANT (Greg ran to)
3. REAGAN (are a gander)
4. PIERCE
   (happier cetacean)
5. FORD (bluff or drop)
6. CARTER
   (Oscar terminally)
7. TAFT (east after)
8. BUSH (Columbus hoped)
9. TRUMAN (diplomat rum and)
10. HOOVER (who over-charged)

Puzzles on page 74.

INDEX

Answer pages are in italics.

WHAT IS AMERICAN MENSA?

American Mensa
The High IQ Society
One out of 50 people qualifies for American Mensa ...
Are YOU the One?

American Mensa, Ltd. is an organization for individuals who have one common trait: a score in the top two percent of the population on a standardized intelligence test. Over five million Americans are eligible for membership ... you may be one of them.

Looking for intellectual stimulation?

You'll find a good "mental workout" in the Mensa Bulletin, our national magazine. Voice your opinion in the newsletter published by your local group. And attend activities and gatherings with fascinating programs and engaging conversation.

Looking for social interaction?

There's something happening on the Mensa calendar almost daily. These range from lectures to game nights to parties. Each year, there are over 40 regional gatherings and the Annual Gathering, where you can meet people, exchange ideas, and make interesting new friends.

Looking for others who share your special interest?

Whether your interest might be computer gaming, the meaning of life, science fiction and fantasy, or scuba diving, there's probably a Mensa Special Interest Group (SIG) for you. There are over 150 SIGs, maintained by members just in the United States.

So visit our Web site for more information about American Mensa Ltd.
http://www.us.mensa.org

Or call our automated messaging system to request an application
or for additional information:
(800) 66-MENSA

Or write to us at:
American Mensa Ltd.
1229 Corporate Drive West
Arlington, TX 76006
AmericanMensa@mensa.org

If you don't live in the United States and would like to get in touch with your national Mensa organization, contact:
Mensa International
15 The Ivories
6-8 Northampton Street,
Islington
London N1 2HY England
www.mensa.org